- Foreword –

With *Courage to Face Anxiety*, I try to help you through your anxiety and panic attacks. Physical symptoms, depression, and agoraphobia are also topics covered in this book. My goal is to make your life easier, to help you enjoy life again, to feel safe and free in your own body, to understand how a panic attack develops, and how you can deal with it. I want to help you accept and reduce your symptoms.

Since I am affected myself, I know the feeling of helplessness that you are probably experiencing. I give you insight into my life with generalized anxiety disorder, panic attacks, agoraphobia, daily symptoms without acute panic attacks, and depression. I also show you how and when things have improved for me. I deliberately say *improved* because I am not fully healed yet.

Nevertheless, it is very important to me that you find a way out of the darkness and experience some relief. Watching others on their healing journey and knowing that recovery is possible has helped me a lot, because I myself could not see the light at the end of the tunnel. I truly felt like I was the only person on this earth going through this. I couldn't understand or explain my symptoms.

So, if you also suffer from one of these conditions or have symptoms without knowing their cause, you have made the right decision to support your healing process with my book. Gather as much information as possible.

Before we begin, I want to make it clear that this book is meant to serve as a guide and is based on my personal experience. I am not a doctor, but someone who is still on their own healing journey.

Fear

Bibliographic Information of the German National Library:
The German National Library lists this publication in the
German National Bibliography; detailed bibliographic data
is available online at dnb.dnb.de.

Publisher: BoD · Books on Demand GmbH, Überseering 33,
22297 Hamburg, bod@bod.de
Printing: Libri Plureos GmbH, Friedensallee 273,
22763 Hamburg

ISBN: 978-3-8482-2809-6

Contents

Definitions and Overview

In the following section, I will explain various topics from A to Z. I will start with anxiety disorders because, for me, they were the most overwhelming. This also includes agoraphobia (social phobia), which is categorized under the different types of anxiety disorders.

Here's an overview:
- Anxiety disorders (Definition, symptoms, causes)
- Physical symptoms (Definition, symptoms, causes)
- Depression (Definition, symptoms, causes)

What Is an Anxiety Disorder?

Anxiety is a natural mechanism of the body that protects us from danger. However, when anxiety becomes excessive, persists for a long time, and significantly impacts daily life, it is classified as an anxiety disorder. This chapter provides an overview of the different aspects of anxiety disorders.

Anxiety disorders are mental health conditions in which individuals suffer from intense and persistent fears. A distinction is made between *healthy anxiety*, which serves a protective function, and pathological anxiety, which is distressing and severely limits quality of life.

Physiology of Anxiety

During a panic attack, our brain reacts as if we were in a life-threatening situation. The amygdala, a part of our limbic system, activates the *fight-or-flight* mode. Stress hormones such as adrenaline and cortisol are released, the heart rate increases, and breathing becomes shallow—all to prepare us for a quick escape. The problem is that our brain triggers this response even in harmless situations, such as when we are out shopping.

There are different types of anxiety disorders, each varying in symptoms and triggers:

Panic Disorder:

Sudden and intense anxiety attacks, often accompanied by physical symptoms such as a racing heart or shortness of breath.

Generalized Anxiety Disorder (GAD):

Persistent and excessive worry about everyday things that is difficult to control (often the fear of fear itself, or the fear of having a panic attack). As a result, this can frequently lead to panic attacks.

Social Phobia, also known as Agoraphobia:

Fear of social situations, especially of negative judgment by others (e.g., fear of crowds, full buses, or events).

Specific Phobias:
Excessive fear of specific objects (e.g., spiders, trains, water) or situations (e.g., flying, snorkeling & diving, conflict, loss, fear of serious health conditions, general poor health, fear of heart attacks and death).

Post-Traumatic Stress Disorder (PTSD):
A reaction to a traumatic experience (e.g., a severe accident, loss, etc.), manifesting through flashbacks, nightmares, and avoidance of triggers (*trigger explanation on page 52*).

Symptoms:
Anxiety disorders manifest on different levels: psychological, physical, and emotional.

Psychological:
Constant worrying, racing thoughts, difficulty concentrating, and forgetfulness. Additionally, irritability becomes noticeable, as the whole experience is exhausting and frustrating.

Physical:
Common symptoms during an anxiety attack include a racing heart, dizziness, sweating, trembling, shortness of breath, nausea, tinnitus, blurred vision, chest tightness, hot and cold flashes, and the feeling of fainting. This can be incredibly frightening, especially during the first experiences.

Emotional:
As if all of this weren't enough, you may feel overwhelmed and helpless in the face of the situation.

Causes:
The causes of anxiety disorders include genetic predisposition, as a family history can increase the risk. Additionally, biological, social, and environmental factors play a significant role. Changes in the brain—especially in neurotransmitters, such as a deficiency in serotonin (*the happiness hormone*)—are also linked to anxiety disorders. Psychological influences, such as childhood neglect or various traumatic experiences, can further contribute to the development of an anxiety disorder.

What Is Depression?

While anxiety disorders are characterized by excessive worry and fear, depression primarily manifests as persistent sadness, lack of motivation, and hopelessness. Both conditions can occur separately or together, significantly impacting the lives of those affected.
Depression can also appear in different forms:

Major Depression:
Persistent depressive episodes with intense sadness, hopelessness, and loss of interest.

Dysthymia (Chronic Depression):
A milder but long-term form of depression.

Bipolar Disorder:
Alternating episodes of depression and mania.

Seasonal Affective Disorder (SAD):
Depressive symptoms that mainly occur during the dark winter months.

Postpartum Depression:
Depression that occurs after childbirth.

Symptoms:
Depression also affects individuals on psychological, physical, and especially emotional levels.

Psychological:
Negative thoughts, hopelessness, and feelings of worthlessness.

Physical & Emotional:
Sleep disturbances, physical exhaustion, loss of appetite, deep sadness, emotional emptiness, and irritability are among the most common symptoms of depression.

Since the causes of depression are often the same as those of anxiety disorders, I will not list them separately again.

What Are Physical Symptoms Without an Acute Panic Attack?

Even without acute panic attacks, anxiety disorders and depression can significantly affect daily life. These subtler symptoms are often overlooked but can be just as distressing:

Constant Inner Restlessness:
A persistent feeling of tension without a clear reason.

Exhaustion:
Even simple tasks like grocery shopping or making phone calls can feel overwhelming.

Difficulty Concentrating:
Thoughts constantly drift, making it hard to stay focused.

Physical Tension:
Muscle tightness, headaches, or a general sense of physical discomfort are common.

Avoidance Behavior:
Avoiding situations or tasks perceived as potentially stressful, even if no acute panic attack is expected.

Feeling Overwhelmed:
Even small decisions or changes in routine can feel insurmountable.

Racing Thoughts:
Overthinking the past or worrying about the future takes up a lot of mental space and prevents a sense of calm.

Dizziness:
A constant or occasional feeling of unsteadiness, often described as a swaying sensation.

Nausea:
Frequently linked to dizziness, persisting as long as the dizziness is present.

Derealization and Brain Fog:
A sense of detachment from the body, blurred perception, feeling like everything is a dream, and difficulty concentrating.

I am also adding my personal symptoms that I have experienced and still experience due to my anxiety disorder:

Trembling, excessive sweating, occasional ringing in the ears, cold-like symptoms, ear pain, hair loss, nervous bladder, intense and uncontrollable itching on the legs, headaches, sleep disturbances, chest tightness.

These symptoms can be persistent (24/7) or appear intermittently. It is essential not only to address acute episodes but also to develop strategies for managing the everyday challenges of anxiety disorders and depression.

Statistics on Anxiety Disorders and Depression :

Prevalence:
Around 10-15% of the population are affected by anxiety disorders, and about 5% suffer from depression.

Combination:
Many people experience both conditions simultaneously, which can complicate diagnosis and treatment.

Age Groups:
Depression and anxiety disorders can occur at any age, but they are especially common during adolescence and young adulthood.

My Story

The Gradual Beginning

I can't even say exactly when and where it all began. In my case, several factors probably came together. I experienced exhaustion, followed by burnout with depression, and finally an anxiety and panic disorder, which eventually became automatic over time. In hindsight, it all seems like a gradual process, accelerated by various events and decisions in my life.

There were numerous triggers in my life that favored these conditions: a toxic relationship, a job that was ultimately bad for me, an environment full of parties and excessive alcohol consumption, and a series of deaths in my circle of friends and family. These experiences left their marks. They burrowed deep into my soul and my body until I finally reached a point where nothing worked anymore. I knew I had to change something if I didn't want to completely break down.

Within a year, I turned my life around completely. I ended the destructive relationship, switched jobs, and sought psychiatric treatment. The hardest step was separating myself from my entire circle of friends. But I knew that everything that was harming me had to disappear from my life. Amidst this chaos, I met my current partner. It was as if life had thrown me a lifeline. We fell in love, and soon after, we moved in together. For the first time in a long while, I felt safe and hopeful. Conclusion: I made a complete fresh start and turned my life upside down.

With this new chapter in life, I also started a new job and was determined to regain control over my life. But then an unexpected event occurred: I had to undergo surgery because a cyst was causing discomfort. It was my first surgery ever, and I was terrified. The thought of losing consciousness and being completely helpless was unbearable for me. As I lay on the operating table, with the mask on my face and anesthesia starting to take effect, I was overwhelmed by a fear of death like I had never experienced before. I felt dizzy, a loud whistling echoed in my ears, and my heart raced. Thoughts like "What if I don't wake up? What if something goes wrong?" were spinning in my mind. Just before I fell asleep, I began to resist, but it was too late.

Waking up from anesthesia was just as traumatic. As I slowly regained consciousness, I heard distorted voices, but I couldn't understand them. Suddenly, I opened my eyes and, as if chased by the devil, scrambled from my operating bed to the recovery bed. Then everything went dark again. More than an hour later, I finally woke up, opened my eyes, and understood where I was: in the recovery room. But immediately, my body began to shake, and I felt ice-cold. I was freezing to the bone, felt weak, and my throat was dry and scratchy. I also felt nauseous and thought I might throw up. But I was too weak to call for help.

After a while, a doctor came and brought me a heating blanket and water. Slowly, my body warmed up, but I sensed that something wasn't right. Shortly after, I was taken to my room.

My partner was by my side and gave me support, but inside, I was battling a wave of fear and despair. The days following the surgery were marked by intense symptoms. Especially at night, the fear became unbearable. Sleepless nights, sweating, and a racing heart kept me awake. That first night after the surgery was a turning point in my life, but not in a positive sense. It marked the beginning of an intense period of suffering.

Even weeks later, I wasn't recovering. The panic attacks became more frequent, and the physical symptoms drained me of all energy. Nausea, which kept me from eating for days, dizziness, and pain accompanied me every day. I was on sick leave for weeks but still tried to push through.
Within two months, my condition deteriorated to the point where I had to go on full sick leave.

It felt as though I had lost all control over my life. I repeatedly visited doctors, convinced that something serious was wrong with my body. But all the tests came back normal. "You're healthy," they told me, but I felt anything but healthy. This discrepancy between what I felt and what the doctors told me almost drove me insane.
In my despair, I finally sought psychiatric help. I was initially diagnosed with depression and admitted to a day clinic. At first, I was full of hope that the structured care and therapy would help me, but after a few weeks, my condition worsened again. The dizziness became a constant companion and deeply unsettled me. Doctors conducted numerous tests, but again, with no result. This lack of answers wore me down.

But there were also moments of light. After my stay in the day clinic, I slowly began to understand my symptoms better. With the help of my therapist, I learned what happens in my body when a panic attack sets in and how I can react to it. It was a slow process, but I started making small improvements. Walks in the forest and various relaxation techniques helped me regulate my nervous system and regain a hint of stability. At the same time, I received a new job, which I would soon start. My employer was informed about my situation and sensitive to it.

My Turning Point

The employment contract had been signed by both parties, and a week before my official start date, I was allowed to get a glimpse into the daily routine. At that time, I was still struggling with severe symptoms and panic attacks—although only about once a week. On my first official workday, I did my best. But soon, I realized that my concentration didn't last long and the physical strain was still too much for me.

Using public transportation was also a huge trigger for me. Despite everything, I managed to get through the day, but as soon as I left the business, I felt worse than ever before. It was a mixture of a bad cold and a panic attack. The train was overcrowded, the bus was the same, and my agoraphobia was extremely tested. Once home, I completely broke down emotionally. I could only cry, felt pain, and was overwhelmed by thoughts that were almost unbearable. As before, I eventually fell asleep from exhaustion—without eating or preparing for bed.

After that night, it felt like everything I had done for my health had been in vain. The daily, hours-long panic attacks returned, making everyday life almost unbearable again. I felt like I was back to square one.

However, this moment became my personal turning point. I decided to pursue a medication treatment with antidepressants, as nothing else seemed to help. Surely, I would have needed more time to make progress naturally, but who has that much time? At the same time, I finally accepted that my mind was sick and that my body reflected that burden. Since a single day of "trial" had been enough to incapacitate me, I asked my employer to cancel the employment contract. This was done with mutual agreement.

Step by Step Back into Life
This acceptance helped me move forward. I learned to better intercept and mitigate my panic attacks, as I began to understand their patterns. I could anticipate how my symptoms would develop and knew what to do when an attack was coming. That gave me a sense of security. I walked a lot in the forest, educated myself about methods to regulate my nervous system, and tried many approaches.

After about four months, I noticed the first improvements when my therapist pointed them out to me. I finally felt secure enough to return to work. As fate would have it, I found a job at a gas station with a 30% workload. I started six months after my turning point.

In those months, I had made so many small but significant improvements that I barely noticed how far I had already come.

Today, more than a year after my turning point, I am getting better step by step. I am still on the road to recovery, but the hopelessness that had accompanied me for so long is gone. My symptoms are still present, but they have become more bearable and no longer disturb me as much as before.

I know the journey is not over yet. Ahead of me lies the task of gradually returning to my learned profession in an office. Still, I am confident. I have learned that healing takes time—but with patience and determination, it is possible.

My Progress Between Turning Point and Now:
- Panic attacks no longer occur daily, but once every six months, the intervals are getting longer.
- I can recognize and prevent panic attacks in many cases.
- If I can't prevent it, I no longer fear a panic attack.
- I went to a restaurant without a panic attack, even several times.
- I dare to go to a city alone.
- Working 30% was not too much.
- I didn't get a panic attack just because I felt sick.
- I went on vacation to a foreign country and had only 3 panic attacks, none lasting longer than 20 minutes.
- I was able to partially process my traumas.

- I have more energy, from permanently "lounging in sweatpants" to dressing nicely and taking care of myself.
- I can sleep through the night—and sleep well.
- I experience more joy again.
- I feel safer in my body again.
- My vision in the dark improved a lot, and I was able to drive again.

Situations from My Everyday Life

Almost every time I went for a walk in the woods, I became dizzy. At first, I didn't know why, and naturally, I started worrying and feeling anxious. Each time, it got a little bit better, so much so that I didn't even notice it. The first walk was tough. I had such dizziness that I thought I would collapse any second. Along with that, a powerful panic attack hit me, with sweating, heart racing, vision problems, trembling, and so on. But I was walking with a group, and I couldn't just turn back. So, I pretended everything was fine. I must have looked pale because the people in the group asked if I was okay. About halfway through, the panic attack and dizziness subsided a little. I was actually able to enjoy the rest of the walk.

If I had turned back, I would have never had that experience because I would have been too scared to go on a walk in the woods alone again.

As mentioned in my story, I had an operation that I was terrified of and went into anesthesia with a panic attack. This led to panic attacks every time I saw a hospital, even from a distance. But I didn't want to let that fear win as well—what would I do if I ever had an accident and didn't want to go to the hospital? I managed to overcome this fear when we visited a family member of my partner in the hospital. It wasn't pleasant, and there were moments when I just wanted to flee. But I didn't, because I wanted to conquer the fear. I walked out of that experience with a clear conscience and felt proud of myself. Even though I was completely drained and exhausted afterward.

For a whole year, I couldn't go back to work. Afterward, I wanted to try with a small workload, even though I feared that after such a tiring day, I would face a setback again. I'm glad I pushed through, and each shift became easier. It wasn't always easy, and I struggled with many symptoms during work, but I never gave up. I took breaks, got some fresh air, but never left work. If I had, I would have proven to my mind that work is dangerous.

Once, a family member told me a not-so-pleasant story from their own life. It was about their struggles and battles they had fought. That directly triggered a panic attack, and I still don't know exactly why to this day. But that's okay; I don't need to know why. I'm a very empathetic person, and sometimes I feel things deeply without meaning to. This attack was very intense and lasted a long time, but I got through it.

My greatest challenge was probably starting my vacation. I was afraid of flying, the house where we would stay, the crowds, the food (since I have celiac disease), the room I would sleep in—basically everything. I consciously decided to go on vacation because I wanted to face my fears once again. It couldn't be that I wouldn't go on vacation just because I was too scared. During these two weeks, I had three panic attacks and several anxiety episodes. But overall, it was somewhat manageable.

My companion, family, and partner were incredibly supportive and understanding, for which I'm very grateful. I often think back to that time and how proud I was when I returned home. I could genuinely say, "I went on vacation," and I'd do it again. Even though now, I would still be a little nervous about it.

Diagnostics and Therapy

First Steps
How do you know if you need help?

As soon as you experience symptoms that have no physical cause, I recommend seeing a therapist. Before that, you should get a thorough examination from a general practitioner to rule out any possible physical causes.

Diagnostic Procedures
What happens with the doctor or therapist?

First, you should visit your general practitioner. Describe your symptoms and have everything tested that could potentially have a physical cause. The doctor will likely take blood samples and have them tested in a lab. You may also be referred to specialists, such as an ENT doctor or neurologist.

If the doctor doesn't find a physical cause, a psychological condition will be considered. At that point, you may be referred to a specialist or you can search for one yourself. It's important that you trust this person and feel safe with them. If you don't feel comfortable with the first therapist, don't hesitate to find another one.

Therapy Methods

Three main therapy methods are generally used:

Psychotherapy:

I highly recommend this, especially if you have little knowledge about how to start addressing your issues. A good psychotherapy session can be incredibly helpful.

Medication:

If the doctor deems it necessary. In my opinion, you should always try the natural route first and only turn to medication if other methods have not worked. This is how I approached it, and I found that medication helped me, although I was initially hesitant. Many people find that medication provides relief.

Alternative Methods:

Mindfulness, meditation, and natural medicine are also very important. A good combination of all these therapy methods can work wonders. For me, mindfulness has played a central role on my journey to recovery.

New Treatment Method: Transcranial Magnetic Stimulation (TMS)

While I was writing this guide, I came across a method for treating depression called Transcranial Magnetic Stimulation (TMS). Here's everything you need to know about it.

How it works:
Transcranial Magnetic Stimulation (TMS) is an innovative, non-invasive treatment method. It uses magnetic fields to stimulate specific brain areas and normalize the brain activity that is often disturbed in depression. A magnetic coil is placed on the patient's head, which generates magnetic pulses that stimulate the underlying nerve cells. The goal is to modulate the activity in brain regions associated with depressive symptoms, improving mood and cognitive control.

Treatment Process:
The treatment typically involves daily sessions over several weeks, with each session lasting about 15 minutes. A newer procedure, called Theta-Burst Stimulation (TBS), allows for even shorter treatment sessions of just a few minutes, and can treat both hemispheres of the brain in one session.

Effectiveness and Tolerability:
Studies show that TMS is an effective and well-tolerated therapy option for patients with depression, especially when other treatment methods have not provided the desired results. Patients often report a noticeable improvement in mood, performance, and control over negative thoughts and feelings.

Current Developments:
In Germany, TMS is already being successfully used at several university hospitals, including those in Tübingen and Greifswald. In Greifswald, the psychiatry and neurology departments are working closely together to offer TMS as a

medication-free and low side-effect therapy for inpatient depression patients.

There are also international advancements: Researchers in Australia have developed a new form of brain stimulation that uses robotics and targeted magnetic stimulation to alter brain activity and communication in patients with depression. This method has shown promising results and is expected to be further studied in state-funded clinical trials in 2025.

Conclusion:
Transcranial Magnetic Stimulation is a promising addition to existing treatment approaches. It offers an effective and well-tolerated alternative, especially for patients who do not respond sufficiently to conventional treatments. If you are interested, it is recommended to consult specialized clinics or experts to learn more about the possibility of TMS treatment.

Coping with Daily Life

You'll now find various coping strategies to overcome your anxiety and panic. I've personally tried many of them. There are numerous tools you can try, and the ones that work best for you should continue to accompany you.

These tools and approaches can be used individually or in combination to alleviate anxiety disorders and depression. Regular use and support from professionals maximize success. Incorporate your favorite tools into your daily life. For each topic, I'll also share my personal experience or opinion. It's important to be patient, as trying something for just one or two weeks won't bring significant progress.

There are indeed many tools, and if the variety feels overwhelming and you're not sure where to start, I completely understand. Start with mindfulness—this is one of the most important tools in my opinion.

You can also try several tools at once, as a combination can increase your success. But don't do too much at once; don't lose focus. Mindfulness can be easily incorporated into your daily life, whether it's at work, in the shopping center, in the woods, on your commute by car or bus.

Second, you can integrate relaxation techniques into your life alongside mindfulness. Try it out and continue until you notice some progress. Then, gradually explore other tools.

If you're already using one or more of these tools, that's awesome!

Keep going!

Psychotherapy

Cognitive Behavioral Therapy (CBT) has proven to be particularly effective. It helps to identify and change negative thought patterns, which can reduce both anxiety and depressive symptoms.

My personal experience:
This strategy helped me a lot because I was educated about my body and its reactions, which allowed me to better understand what was happening and how to deal with it. For me, this form of therapy was one of the most important, as I could always rely on the collaboration with my therapist.

If you're still looking for a therapist, don't be discouraged if you don't connect with the first person. Keep searching. It is really important that you can speak openly and honestly about your problems and fears. Therapy where you don't feel comfortable because you're afraid of being judged or something else is not beneficial and won't help you or the therapist.

You will be helped and supported by a professional who surely has experience and has accompanied people like you on their healing journey.

Relaxation Techniques

Relaxation techniques help release physical tension and promote inner calm. They can be applied regularly or in acute stress situations. Methods:

Progressive Muscle Relaxation (PMR):
Technique: Alternating tensing and relaxing individual muscle groups. Perform the exercise usually while sitting or lying down. You can find guided PMR exercises on YouTube. Effect: Relieves muscular tension and calms the nervous system.

My personal experience:
This technique initially triggered panic in me because my mind told me that relaxation was dangerous. If this is also the case for you, keep going. Once you teach your brain that resting is not harmful, it can really help you relax and even sleep.

Body Scan:
Technique: A conscious awareness and relaxation of all body areas. Feel your body and mentally focus on each body part. What do I feel in my right arm, for example? Is it tingling, or does it feel light? Notice any tension, especially in the chest, abdomen, and especially the shoulders and neck. Effect: Promotes body awareness and relieves tension.

My personal experience:
I personally suffered from the fear of suddenly having a heart attack or cancer, etc. A slight pain in the chest led to a spiral of thoughts, eventually resulting in a panic attack. The body scan technique helped me regulate the overwhelming need to control my body. This means no more checking my pulse, no more googling what my symptoms might mean for my health, and most importantly, much less fear of sudden health deterioration.

Visualization (Imagination):
Technique: Mentally transport yourself to a safe or pleasant place.
Effect: Helps replace negative thoughts and creates a positive mood.

My personal experience:
I tried this technique once, and unfortunately, it didn't work for me. My anxiety disorder made it difficult to imagine, and I couldn't focus on picturing a safe place. At that time, I also didn't understand why I should imagine a safe place. However, it has improved since then. I haven't consciously practiced visualization again, but it sounds relaxing and might be worth trying again.

Yoga:
Technique: A combination of breathing exercises, stretches, and mindfulness. There are many guided yoga sessions available on YouTube.
Effect: Reduces stress, strengthens the body, and promotes inner balance.

My personal experience:
I tried yoga once or twice. For someone who has little to no stamina, it can be very exhausting at first, which can be intimidating. But it really benefits the body, and you feel it after a few sessions. I highly recommend it!

Sleep Relaxation:
Technique: Relaxation techniques specifically before going to sleep (e.g., PMR or calming sounds). You can find a lot of these on YouTube.
Effect: Improves sleep and helps with nighttime restlessness.

My personal experience:
Before going to sleep, I like to listen to an artist named Adam, who plays handpans and tangrams. You can find him on Spotify under ethereal.in.e. I find it very calming. As mentioned in the Progressive Muscle Relaxation section, I sometimes fell asleep during the exercise. Don't be discouraged if you can't fall asleep immediately or if your sleep disorders aren't fixed right away—it takes time. If it helps you, keep going.

Mindfulness:
Mindfulness techniques help you stay in the present moment and prevent negative thoughts and feelings from overwhelming you. Methods:

    Meditation:
    Technique: Focused attention (e.g., on the breath, a mantra, or sounds).

Variants:

> Guided meditation: Accompanied by instructions.
> Silent meditation: Done independently.
> Loving-kindness meditation: Cultivates compassion for oneself and others.
> Effect: Promotes serenity and clarity.

My personal experience:
Guided meditation is especially helpful at first, as not everyone knows how a meditation should unfold. If you can focus entirely on the exercise, it's very calming and creates overall clarity in your mind.

Silent meditation, I would say, is for more advanced practitioners who understand how meditation works and have already tried guided meditations. For me, the effects weren't as noticeable with silent meditation as they were with guided ones.

As I mentioned, I had difficulty concentrating, so I found it hard to focus on the meditation by myself in silence. But if you master it, it can be truly freeing and relax your mind.

Loving-kindness meditation:
I've never tried this one. It sounds like a very emotional topic, which could lead to emotional outbursts, especially for people with trauma. This can be good because avoiding emotions should be avoided—it can promote anxiety and depression.

Mindful Breathing:
Technique: Focus on the breath without judgment. Feel how the breath flows into your lungs and then out.
Effect: Shifts attention away from worries and into the present moment.

My personal experience:
Focusing on your breath can be difficult, especially in the middle of a panic attack, as you think about everything except calming down. However, it's a great coping strategy when you fear a panic attack is approaching. It helps you feel grounded.

Mindful Eating:
Technique: Eating slowly and mindfully to notice taste, texture, and smell.
Effect: Reduces stress and encourages healthy eating habits.

My personal experience:
Mindful eating and drinking are very important. Many people are used to doing everything quickly, especially in today's fast-paced society. Take the time to enjoy your meal. Savor it mindfully.

Mindful Observation:
Technique: Notice the environment or inner sensations without judgment.
Effect: Builds the ability to accept thoughts and emotions without identifying with them.

My personal experience:
Conscious observation has helped me come back to reality when I was staring into space. It can be very interesting to consciously observe.

5-4-3-2-1 Technique:
Technique: Name 5 things you see, 4 you feel, 3 you hear, 2 you smell, and 1 you taste.
Effect: Grounds you and calms you in moments of acute anxiety.

My personal experience:
As the effect suggests, this technique helps during an acute panic attack. It has helped me countless times to break free from my panic, confuse my brain, and escape the cycle.

Mindful Walking:
Technique: Slow, conscious walking, focusing on steps and the body.
Effect: Promotes movement and mental clarity.

My personal experience:
I really enjoy mindful walking and feeling my body because often you walk like a zombie with a great emptiness. You don't feel right in your body. This awareness helps with dizziness and brain fog.

Physical Activities:
Regular exercise has been proven to reduce anxiety and depression by releasing endorphins and improving general well-being. Some effective approaches are:

Endurance sports:
Running, cycling, or swimming promote the release of mood-enhancing neurotransmitters like serotonin and dopamine.

My personal experience:
Walking in the woods was always helpful for me, as was jogging, but I mostly just walked. I did this daily, starting with ten minutes a day and gradually increasing to three hours daily. It helped me most to connect with nature, which can be very healing.

Yoga:
Combinations of movement, breathing control, and meditation can reduce stress and anxiety. Studies show yoga is particularly helpful for anxiety disorders.

My personal opinion:
I've never really practiced yoga, but I would like to. There are guided yoga sessions on YouTube. Yoga also helps "healthy" people stay fit and healthy.

Dancing or rhythmic movement:
Not only does it promote physical fitness, but it also improves emotional regulation.

My personal experience:
During my stay at the day clinic, we had a motor skills lesson, and at the end, we always learned a group dance. At that time, it triggered a panic attack for me because the spinning and jumping movements made my dizziness worse. It's no longer a problem for me, but I haven't tried it again yet.

Exposure Therapy:
Exposure therapy is a central component ofcognitive-behavioral therapy (CBT) and helps overcome fears by systematically and repeatedly exposing you to anxiety-inducing situations:

> **Graduated Exposure:**
> Start with less stressful situations and work your way up to more intense ones.

My personal experience:
Facing fear is just part of the process for me because you will never get rid of it if you don't confront it. I started with small things and gradually exposed myself to greater fears and discomforts. It didn't always go as planned, and there were setbacks, but that's okay. You can't expect it to work every time. What's important is that you don't get discouraged and try again.

Flooding:
Direct confrontation with the most fear-inducing situation to reduce the fear response.

My personal experience:
This method didn't work well for me. I tried it too early in my healing process. I consciously decided not to use this method. However, some people have been helped by flooding.

Virtual Reality (VR):
Increasingly used in exposure therapy to safely simulate anxiety-inducing scenarios.

My personal opinion:
I don't have an experience with virtual reality, as I've never tried it and probably won't. I often get very dizzy with visual inconsistencies and headaches. I also prefer reality. On the other hand, the technology has advanced a lot, so if you're curious, give it a try!

Medication Therapy:
In some cases, antidepressants or anti-anxiety medications may be useful, especially if other measures are not effective. The decision to take medication should always be made in consultation with a doctor.

My personal experience:
I always got very anxious thinking about taking antidepressants. I wanted to stick it out, but I eventually realized that it was necessary. It's okay to ask for help, whether through therapy or medication. Your healing journey is unique, and it's okay if medication is part of it.

Medication Therapy:
In some cases, antidepressants or anxiolytic medications can be beneficial, especially when other measures are insufficient. The decision to use medication should always be made in consultation with healthcare professionals.

My personal experience:
I always felt a strong aversion to the idea of taking antidepressants. I wanted to stick to the natural path. As you can read in my story, I eventually agreed to give SSRIs a chance. I was definitely terrified of the side effects and hesitated for a long time before taking them. But when I reached my lowest point and couldn't go on, I had no choice. The only thing that could get me out of that hole were the medications. As is well known, the effects take a few weeks to kick in, and I did feel them. Antidepressants definitely helped me, but how much, I cannot say. Whether it was a combination of the medication and my change in perspective on the anxiety disorder, I will probably never find out.

Social Support:
The feeling of not being alone strengthens resilience.

Self-Help Groups:
Group meetings allow you to exchange experiences with others who are facing similar challenges and offer emotional support.

Benefits:

> **Experience exchange:** Participants learn strategies that have helped others.

> **Local and online groups:** Many self-help groups also offer virtual meetings, such as those provided by organizations like [insert organization name here].

My personal experience:
The above three points all lead in the same direction for me. Opening up and being willing to listen to others can change and improve your perspective on certain fears or attitudes. My best friend and I were both diagnosed with an anxiety disorder at the same time, and fortunately, we were able to exchange and support each other. There are so many people who suffer from mental illnesses and are afraid to talk about them in public because they fear being judged or not taken seriously. I know that feeling as well. There are people who don't want to understand or are not interested; that's okay, you can deliberately ignore them.

Healthy Lifestyle:
A healthy lifestyle is crucial for mental health:

Nutrition:
A balanced diet rich in fruits, vegetables, whole grains, and omega-3 fatty acids supports brain health and can reduce feelings of anxiety.

My personal experience:
Nutrition is very important for a healthy life. During the tests I underwent, I was diagnosed with celiac disease. This is a gluten intolerance and can have serious consequences when consuming gluten-containing foods. Acute symptoms such as abdominal pain, diarrhea, nausea, and vomiting are common in this autoimmune disease. As a result, I switched to a completely gluten-free diet and have been very careful about eating healthily ever since. Less sugar, more vegetables and fruits, less caffeine, and no alcohol. Every day I cooked and still cook fresh meals. If you stick with it for a while, you'll quickly notice changes such as more energy, clearer thinking, and generally improved fitness.

Sleep:
Getting enough sleep (7-9 hours per night) is essential for reducing stress and improving cognitive function.

My personal experience:
Many people with anxiety disorders and depression also suffer from sleep disturbances. Possible causes include racing thoughts, manifested fears, and general inner restlessness. However, if you can sleep well, it is very important to allow yourself those eight hours of sleep. In my healing process, I could hardly sleep for weeks, if not months. And when I did manage to sleep, it felt like I had just laid there with my eyes closed all night. Now, I no longer have any sleep issues.

Avoiding Alcohol and Nicotine:
These substances can exacerbate feelings of anxiety.

My personal experience:
I don't think much needs to be said about this, as alcohol and nicotine consumption is generally not considered healthy. My excessive alcohol consumption certainly contributed to my anxiety. When I changed my environment, I abruptly stopped drinking alcohol. I don't regret that decision one bit. Unfortunately, I've been a smoker for years and haven't yet been able to quit nicotine. I think avoiding other intoxicating substances is self-explanatory.

Autogenic Training:
Autogenic training is a relaxation technique that uses self-suggestion to bring about physiological and psychological relaxation.

Basic principles:

Heaviness exercise:
Focus: "My arms and legs are heavy."
Effect: Muscle relaxation and feeling of calm.

Warmth exercise:
Focus: "My arms and legs are warm."
Effect: Promotes circulation and warmth sensation.

Heart exercise:
Focus: "My heart beats calmly and regularly."
Effect: Regulates heart rate and reduces palpitations due to anxiety.

Breathing exercise:
Focus: "My breath flows calmly and evenly."
Effect: Calms breathing and relieves tension.

Abdomen or solar plexus exercise:
Focus: "My stomach is pleasantly warm."
Effect: Relieves abdominal discomfort and reduces tension.

Cool forehead exercise:
Focus: "My forehead is pleasantly cool."
Effect: Promotes clarity in the head and reduces headaches.

Extensions:

Formula-based intentions: For example, "I am calm and composed" as a recurring suggestion.

Individual visualizations: A pleasant image or calming scene as a focus.

My personal experience:
The seven techniques mentioned above are very relaxing, and I perform them daily when I am calm and relaxed. You can also, when you sense a panic attack coming, choose

one of these exercises, sit in front of a mirror, and calmly but consciously talk to yourself. It helped me, especially when I was alone and feeling nervous, restless, and uncomfortable inside.

Breathing Techniques:
Breathing techniques help calm the nervous system, reduce stress, and gain control over physical symptoms of anxiety. They regulate oxygen intake and have a calming effect on the body.

Methods:
Diaphragmatic Breathing:
Technique: Breathe deeply into your abdomen, not your chest. Inhale through your nose, push your belly out, and exhale through your mouth. Effect: Activates the parasympathetic nervous system, promotes relaxation.

Box Breathing:
Technique: Inhale for 4 seconds, hold for 4 seconds, exhale for 4 seconds, pause for 4 seconds. Effect: Stabilizes breathing and calms the mind.

4-7-8 Breathing Technique:
Technique: Inhale for 4 seconds, hold for 7 seconds, exhale for 8 seconds.
Effect: Effective for sleep problems and acute anxiety.

Alternate Nostril Breathing (Nadi Shodhana):
Technique: Breathe alternately through one nostril at a time, closing the other with your finger.
Effect: Promotes inner balance and clarity.

Slow Counting:
Technique: Count while inhaling and exhaling (e.g., up to 5).
Effect: Focuses the mind and calms thoughts.

Pursed Lip Breathing:
Technique: Inhale slowly through the nose and exhale through slightly pursed lips.
Effect: Lengthens the exhalation and reduces feelings of breathlessness.

My personal experience:
Breathing techniques helped me calm down and reduce my pulse during acute panic attacks. My favorite is the 4-7-8 breathing technique. I also used diaphragmatic breathing to alleviate dizziness. In general, I recommend everyone find their favorite breathing technique and practice it daily, whether or not they're experiencing an acute panic attack. I liked using it during morning walks in the forest.

Additional Tools I Used Daily:

Humming:
Activates the vagus nerve and contributes to overall relaxation and anxiety relief.

Positive Self-Influence:
Stand in front of the mirror every morning and tell yourself that it's going to be a good day, and that you will handle whatever comes your way. Tell yourself that you're feeling good, you look good, and you will confidently step out of the house.

Power Sport:
Jumping or running in place for three minutes during an acute panic attack to raise your heart rate and then lower it back to normal.

EFT Tapping:
EFT tapping involves stimulating various acupuncture points following a specific pattern.

> **Effect of EFT:**
> Tapping is combined with affirmations. This helps release internal blockages, such as anxiety, and reduce stress. You can find the tapping points easily. EFT tapping is ideal for self-application because you don't need to hit the points precisely—unlike acupuncture, where the needles must be placed exactly on the relevant meridian points. EFT tapping can release blockages even if

you're just tapping in the general area of the points. Check online or watch YouTube videos for guidance.

Distraction:

I would end the mental carousel or anxious thoughts by simply continuing with my usual activities, such as household chores, gaming, walking, crocheting, reading, etc. Always make sure not to try to suppress the thoughts forcefully but just change your focus.

Daily Routines:

Incorporate routines into your daily life, like facial care in the morning or stretching exercises. Something that helps you wake up. Personally, I found facial care very helpful, and I also used ice for a refreshing effect. A cold shower would also be a good idea.

Small Projects:

Similar to distraction, I engaged in small projects to stay occupied. My projects included seasonal redecorating, small crochet projects, making gifts (handmade dreamcatchers), reading books, reorganizing chaotic cupboards or shelves, beauty days or wellness days at home, shopping with the intention of finding something nice for myself.

Online Programs and Apps:

Digital offerings provide structured self-help programs that can support individuals in managing their anxiety. Studies show positive effects of such applications.

Digital Tools offer flexible and affordable self-help options:

Online therapy platforms: Programs like Selfapy, HelloBetter, and deprexis combine CBT approaches with interactive elements.

Apps:

Headspace: For meditation and mindfulness.

Calm: Promotes sleep and stress reduction.

MindShift: Specifically for anxiety management.

MindDoc: For daily reflection and mood tracking.

Insight Timer: Guided meditations specifically for anxiety.

Self-Help Materials:

Books like *"Therapy Tools for Anxiety Disorders"* by Silka Hagena and Malte Gebauer offer diagnostic and therapeutic materials for personal use. Self-help literature and materials can support the management of anxiety disorders:

"The Anxiety and Phobia Workbook" by Edmund J. Bourne.

"Mind Over Mood" by Dennis Greenberger and Christine Padesky.

"Anxiety A to Z" by Tamryn J. Burgers, R.H.N. *"Understanding and Overcoming Anxiety"* by Doris Wolf.

Workbooks: Many CBT workbooks offer structured exercises to manage anxiety.

Online Resources: Websites like Mind.org andPsychCentral.com offer practical tips and information.

Recognizing Triggers

Meaning in Different Contexts:

Psychology & Trauma:
A trigger can be a memory, sound, smell, or situation that provokes a strong emotional reaction. Especially in conditions like PTSD (Post-Traumatic Stress Disorder) or anxiety disorders, triggers can provoke symptoms such as panic, flashbacks, or dissociation. Example: Someone who has experienced a car accident might be triggered by squealing tires or loud engine noises.

General Emotional Triggers:
Even without trauma, people can have triggers that activate unpleasant emotions, such as certain words, behaviors, or memories.
Example: A derogatory remark can trigger old insecurities and cause stress or anxiety.

Internet & Social Media:
The term "triggering" is often used when content or statements provoke strong emotional reactions, especially on sensitive topics. Trigger warnings are common to prepare people when a topic might be emotionally distressing (e.g., content related to trauma, violence, or mental health issues).

Physiological Triggers: Sometimes physical stimuli can act as triggers, like caffeine triggering panic attacks or flickering lights causing migraines.

How to Recognize Triggers and Deal with Them:

Keeping a Daily Journal can help you identify triggers and patterns. Triggers can be diverse and unique to each individual. They often arise from a combination of external influences, internal thoughts, or physical sensations. Common examples include:

> **Situational Triggers:** Certain places, like confined spaces or crowds.

> **Emotional Triggers:** Stress, feeling overwhelmed, or conflicts.

> **Physical Sensations:** Heart palpitations, dizziness, or shortness of breath that can intensify the anxiety spiral.

> **Cognitive Triggers:** Negative self-talk, memories of traumatic events, or worries about the future.

To better identify triggers, the following strategies can help:

> **Self-Observation:** As mentioned earlier, keep a journal to document situations, thoughts, and physical reactions.

> **Noticing Physical Signals:** Pay attention to signs such as sweating, trembling, or changes in breathing. Dizziness, stomach pain, or nausea can indeed trigger anxiety disorders.

Recognizing Patterns: Are there recurring situations or topics that trigger anxiety? For example, whenever I felt nauseous for any reason, my fear of vomiting would quickly escalate into a severe panic attack.

Dealing with Triggers

Once triggers are identified, targeted strategies can help manage them:

Acute Strategies for the Moment:
> **Breathing Exercises:**
> Focus on slow, deep breathing (e.g., your favorite breathing technique). This helps calm the nervous system.
>
> **Grounding Techniques:**
> Shift your attention to the present moment by, for example, counting objects in the room or feeling the ground beneath your feet. The 5-4-3-2-1 technique works wonderfully here.
>
> **Calming Self-Talk:**
> Remind yourself that the anxiety is temporary and there is no real danger. Recognize that your brain has activated a false alarm, thinking you're in danger. It's trying to protect you. Use techniques like the breathing exercise to show both your brain and body that you're safe.

Long-Term Coping: Building Resilience
Confronting fear and panic is challenging but also an opportunity to strengthen resilience — your inner strength. Learn to view your triggers as signals of underlying needs. For example, an anxiety response might indicate that you need more rest, boundaries, or support.

Conclusion:

Recognizing and dealing with triggers takes time, patience, and practice. The key is mindfulness of your reactions and being willing to experiment with constructive strategies. With the right support and ongoing practice, you can learn to regain control over your fears and live a fulfilling life.

Building a Support Network: The Role of Friends, Family, and Support Groups

A strong and supportive network can play a crucial role in coping with anxiety disorders. Isolation is often a companion to anxiety and depression, and building a stable social support system can help counteract it.

Friends, family, or like-minded people can offer comfort and understanding in difficult times. A supportive environment serves as a reminder that progress is possible, even when setbacks occur. Accompanying you to doctor's appointments, helping with daily tasks, or simply offering a listening ear can be incredibly valuable. Dealing with a mental health condition can make you feel isolated enough already.

Explaining the Disorder:
It can be helpful to explain to your loved ones what an anxiety disorder is and how it manifests. Many people don't fully understand what happens during these moments and may need guidance on how they can help.

Setting Boundaries:
Also, set clear boundaries. Share what helps and what doesn't. It's essential that the support matches your needs. Unfortunately, there are many cases where people with mental health conditions are not taken seriously—even by family members. Sometimes, it's not possible to change the beliefs or attitudes of others, even if you wish to. It's

important to recognize that their reactions say more about them than they do about you or your condition. This doesn't make your experiences any less valid or real. If your family is not supportive, focus on people who understand and can offer support—friends, self-help groups, therapists, and online communities. These are all avenues to find people who are willing to understand and support you.

Distance When Necessary:
If you find that conversations with your family are damaging to your mental health, it's okay to distance yourself. Although it's hard to cope without family support, you can still make progress.

When Family Wants to Help:
Sometimes, family members want to help but don't know how. Simple suggestions like, "Can you remind me to take regular breaks?" can be useful.

Maintaining a Network:
Building a network is just the first step—maintaining it is equally important. Show gratitude and appreciation for the support you receive from others. Small gestures, such as a quick call or meeting up, help keep the connection alive. Make sure you also listen and support others. It should be a give-and-take relationship that strengthens the bond.

Children and Adolescents with Anxiety Disorders:
For children, anxiety can feel uncontrollable because they may not have the tools to cope with it. I remember feeling my heart race as a child before giving a presentation. Back

then, no one could have explained to me that it was "just anxiety." Parents should learn to recognize their children's signals and guide them gently.

How Family Members Can Support:
Family members often ask, "What can I do?" My answer is: Listen. Don't focus on finding solutions—just be there. Sometimes, simply saying, "I'm here for you" is enough. At the same time, family members should avoid overloading themselves. Their role is not to heal but to offer support.

Stigmatization:
The most common prejudice I've encountered is: "Just pull yourself together." These words can be hurtful and demotivating. However, they often reflect a lack of understanding. Openness and conversations are key to overcoming such misconceptions.

Self-Care: The Key to Healing and Stability

Self-care is a central aspect of coping with anxiety disorders. It is more than just a nice extra—it is the foundation for strengthening oneself, building resources, and establishing a mindful approach to mental health in the long term. It involves taking active responsibility for your own well-being and consciously setting aside time for yourself. Another word for this is mindfulness—treating yourself with care.

Why is Self-Care Important?

People like you and me often tend to neglect ourselves. The inner critic can become loud, the desire to please others outweighs our own needs, or we feel paralyzed by the symptoms of anxiety. However, it is precisely during these moments that it is essential to engage consciously with yourself and do something kind for yourself. Self-care helps reduce stress levels, strengthen resilience, and improve your relationship with yourself. It is not selfish; it is a necessity for staying healthy in the long term.

Self-Acceptance:

The most important step in my journey was the realization that I didn't need to be "fixed." I am not broken. Anxiety is a part of me, and even though it is not always welcome, it has shown me how strong I am. Self-acceptance does not mean loving the anxiety, but accepting it without letting it define you. My favorite analogy here is: An anxiety disorder or depression is like a stray dog that follows you. You can't just shoo it away. It follows you everywhere. Now, you choose to accept the dog that follows you. You take care of it, you nurture it, and you tend to it. It is now part of you, and you no longer want it to leave.

What Does Self-Care Look Like in Everyday Life?

Self-care is as individual as each person. There is no universal recipe, but some tried-and-tested approaches can help make everyday life more mindful. My formula mainly includes physical movement in the form of walks, plenty of sleep, healthy eating, gradually facing my anxiety, and wellness or beauty days.

Promoting Physical Health:

A balanced diet, enough sleep, and regular exercise have a positive impact on mental health. Walks in the fresh air, yoga, or a relaxing bath can work wonders.

Finding Emotional Balance:

Allowing feelings to arise and giving them space is an important part of self-care. Journaling or talking to someone trusted can help sort and process emotions.

Setting Boundaries:

Saying "no" is often hard, but clear boundaries are necessary to protect yourself. Learn not to overwhelm yourself and recognize that it's okay to prioritize your own needs.

Establishing Routines:
A structured day provides stability and security. Intentionally set aside time for relaxation, creative activities, or simply to "be" without pressure.

Practicing Mindfulness:
Practices like meditation, breathing techniques, or mindful eating can help you stay in the moment and break the cycle of overthinking.

Obstacles on the Path to Self-Care:
For many, self-care feels unfamiliar or even uncomfortable at first. Guilt or the belief that there is no time for yourself can create obstacles. But it is worth persevering. Small steps, like taking a moment to rest or reading an inspiring book, can be the start of a loving relationship with yourself.

Conclusion: An Act of Self-Love
Self-care is an expression of self-love and a powerful tool in coping with anxiety disorders. It not only helps alleviate acute symptoms but also strengthens the foundation for stable mental health. Start with small steps and make self-care a permanent part of your life. You are worth giving yourself the same attention and care that you offer to others.

The Road Ahead

The journey through an anxiety disorder is often challenging and demands a lot of patience and courage. However, just as there are difficult moments, this path also offers the opportunity to grow, to get to know yourself better, and to develop a new perspective on life. This chapter is about looking forward to the future with confidence, understanding setbacks as part of the process, and encouraging others that healing is possible.

Setbacks and Progress: Healing is Not a Linear Process
There is a widespread belief that healing is a straight line—from pain to stability, with no detours. I once wished for this too. But in reality, healing is often more like a roller coaster ride. Setbacks are not failures, but part of the growth process. They remind us that change takes time and that we can always start over.
It can be helpful to see setbacks as an opportunity to pause and reflect. What stressors or triggers caused the setback? What have I learned from previous experiences that can help me now? What progress have I made that I shouldn't lose sight of?

The most important thing is not to despair after a setback and not to give up. Every small step counts, and even apparent setbacks can provide valuable lessons for the journey ahead. Setbacks may manifest in the form of more frequent panic attacks, a few days of intense dizziness (after, for example, a very good week with almost no symptoms), constant nausea, or any other symptoms reappearing stronger. That's okay, and it will pass.

Positive Changes: Growth Through Difficult Times
Even though anxiety disorders are often marked by pain and frustration, they can lead to positive changes in the long run. Many people report that their experiences with anxiety have given them a deeper understanding of themselves and others. You can experience this too. Here are some of the positive aspects you might discover on your journey:

> **Stronger Self-Awareness:** You learn to pay more attention to yourself and to respect your needs.

> **Appreciation of Small Moments:** The journey out of anxiety often shows how important little, everyday joys are. A sunny day, a good conversation, or a moment of peace can suddenly feel much more meaningful.

> **Empathy for Others:** Your experiences make you more sensitive to the struggles that others go through, and you may develop a deeper compassion.

These changes are like milestones that show that you have not only survived but have also grown internally. Keep track of every small progress, whether it's through a photo or by writing it down. Remind yourself of these moments when you have a bad day.

Motivation for Others: Sharing Hope

One of the most valuable realizations along the way through anxiety is that you are not alone, and you never were. Your story can inspire others who are just beginning their journey or are going through a particularly tough moment. Just like I am doing now, even though I am not completely healed, I have still made remarkable progress and want to share my experiences and insights with you so that you too can escape your cycle of anxiety.

Conclusion: Your Path, Your Strength

The road ahead is a road full of possibilities. Even though challenges may still arise, you have already proven strength and resilience through your journey. Believe that every step you take is a step toward healing—even if it seems small.

Remember, you don't have to be perfect. You are already enough, just as you are. And by walking this path, you are not only doing yourself a favor—you are also inspiring others to overcome their own fears and look forward to the future with courage.

You are the proof that healing is possible. Let us look forward together—full of hope, courage, and confidence.

Positive Affirmations

Stand in front of a mirror and speak kindly to yourself. Below are some affirmations that can positively influence your day:

Self-Acceptance and Self-Love:
"I am enough as I am."
"My feelings are valid, and I am allowed to feel them."
"It's okay not to be perfect."
"I accept myself with all my strengths and weaknesses."
"I deserve love, respect, and understanding."

Building Self-Confidence:
"I have the strength to overcome difficult times."
"Every challenge makes me stronger."
"I am brave and grow with every experience."
"My worth does not depend on my performance."
"I have already achieved so much, and I will master this as well."

Coping with Anxiety:
"My anxiety does not define me."
"I am safe and in control of my body."
"I let the anxiety come and go without judging it."
"I am stronger than my thoughts and feelings."
"I breathe deeply and let calmness flow into my body."

Relieving Depression:

"It's okay to accept help."
"Each day offers a new chance for hope."
"I find light, even when it seems dark."
"My life has meaning, even when I can't always see it."
"Small steps lead me to a better tomorrow."

Promoting Mindfulness:

"I am safe in the here and now."
"Every breath brings me calm and clarity."
"I take each moment as it comes without judgment."
"My body and mind deserve rest and peace."
"I appreciate the beauty in small things around me."

Motivation for Change:

"Every small progress is a big step in the right direction."
"I am on the path to healing, and I allow myself time."
"I allow myself to let go of the old and welcome the new."
"I deserve to be happy."
"My life is worth being filled with joy."

Motivating and Empowering Quotes for You Write down the ones you like on a note and stick it somewhere you see every day.

Courage and Hope:
> "Fear is the constant companion of courage." – Unknown
> "Life begins where fear ends." – Osho
> "Courage is not the absence of fear, but the overcoming of fear." – Nelson Mandela
> "In the deepest moments of despair, a spark of hope can change everything." – Unknown
> "A small step in the right direction can be the biggest of your life." – Unknown
> "Even clouds with dark skies cannot stay forever." – Unknown
> "If you're going through hell, keep going." – Winston Churchill

Acceptance and Self-Love:
> "I am not perfect, and that's okay." – Unknown
> "Self-love means embracing yourself even on bad days." – Unknown
> "It's not your job to be perfect. It's your job to be yourself." – Unknown
> "The strongest weapon against self-doubt is self-acceptance." – Unknown
> "You are enough, just as you are." – Unknown
> "Your feelings are valid, no matter how they look." – Unknown

"Be patient with yourself. Healing takes time." –
Unknown

Overcoming Difficulties:

"Sometimes we don't know how strong we are until being strong is the only choice." – Bob Marley
"Even from stones that are thrown in your way, you can build something beautiful." – Erich Kästner
"After every storm comes a rainbow." – Unknown
"The dark makes the light visible." – Unknown
"Your worst day lasts only 24 hours." – Unknown
"Don't forget: It's okay to take breaks. It doesn't mean you give up." – Unknown
"The path may be rocky, but every step brings you closer to the goal." – Unknown

Mindfulness and Living in the Moment:

"Breathe in. Breathe out. This is a moment, not a permanent state." – Unknown
"The here and now is the only place where you truly live." – Thich Nhat Hanh
"Take time to see the little things – they are the greatest." – Unknown
"The moment you give yourself time is a moment of healing." – Unknown
"Every breath is a new chance to start over." – Unknown
"Don't rush to fix everything at once. Sometimes it's just about taking one breath at a time." – Unknown

On Hope and Healing:

"Hope is the light that never goes out, even in the darkest night." – Unknown

"It may not be easy, but it will be worth it." – Unknown

"Sometimes the path only reveals itself when you take the first step." – Unknown

"There's always a second chance. It's called tomorrow." – Unknown

"Every scar tells the story of a battle you've survived." – Unknown

"Sometimes healing means accepting that not every day will be good." – Unknown

"Your present self is stronger than your past self." – Unknown

Motivation and Strength:

"Don't give up, because you are stronger than you think." – Unknown

"Even small progress is progress." – Unknown

"Growth rarely happens in the comfort zone." – Unknown

"It's not the mountain you have to conquer, but yourself." – Edmund Hillary

"What's hard today will become your strength tomorrow." – Unknown

"The greatest strength often lies in the ability to keep going." – Unknown

"You are not alone. There are people who understand and want to support you." – Unknown

Small Reminders:

> "A bad day doesn't mean a bad life." – Unknown
> "It's okay to be tired. Allow yourself to rest." – Unknown
> "Take the days as they come. Tomorrow is a new chance." – Unknown
> "Allow yourself to make mistakes. That means you're trying." – Unknown
> "You are not your fear – you are so much more." – Unknown
> "Sometimes courage means just getting up and trying again." – Unknown

These quotes can inspire, strengthen, and guide you. They can be written in journals, repeated as daily affirmations, or turned into small cards to remind yourself every day that healing is possible.

Graphics and Diagrams

A picture speaks more than a thousand words – and this is true even when dealing with anxiety disorders. Graphics and illustrations can present complex concepts in a clear and accessible way, and can support the healing process. In this chapter, I'll show how diagrams and quotes not only provide guidance but can also serve as motivation.

Diagrams and inspiring quotes are more than just visual elements – they are tools that help us understand anxiety and healing. They offer direction, motivation, and hope, and can be used anywhere along the journey where a little extra support is needed.

This is meant to encourage you not just to read, but to actively reflect and engage – whether by creating your own diagrams or collecting your favorite quotes. Every journey begins with a first step – and a clear vision of where it is going.

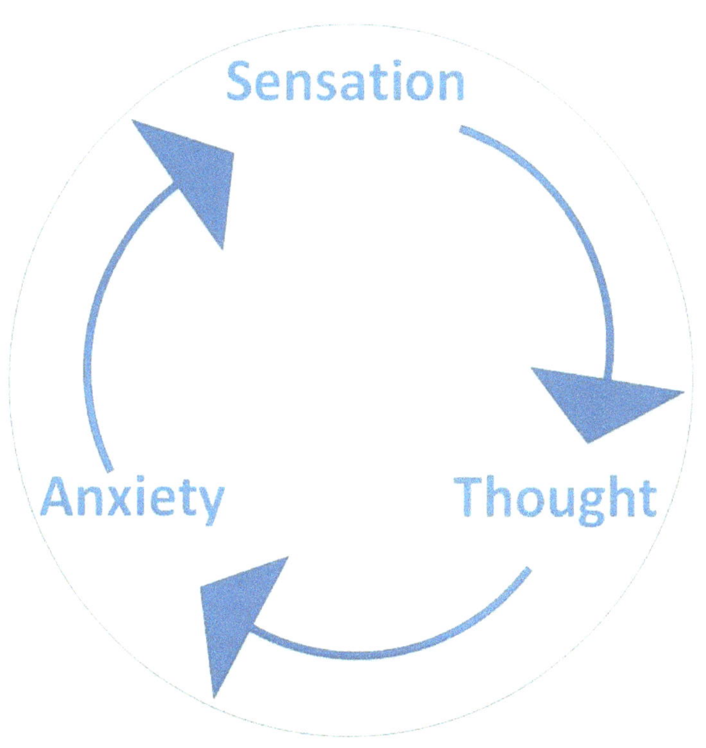

Sensation
Thought
Anxiety

Acknowledgements

There are moments in life when, without the support and belief of others, we cannot move forward. This book would not have been possible without the people who stood by my side.

My deepest gratitude goes to my partner. You have been my rock in the storm, my anchor during turbulent times, and my unwavering support, even when I felt lost. Your patience, love, and belief in me have given me more strength than words can express. I love you ♥

A heartfelt thank you also goes to my family and my partner's family. Your support, understanding, and belief in me have given me hope during tough times. Thank you for always being there for me and making me feel that I was never alone. A special thanks to my mother, who helped me with the creation of this book and supported me wholeheartedly. Thank you, Mom ♥

To my best friend, I am deeply grateful for all the hours you've listened to me, encouraged me, and reminded me that I am stronger than I think. You reminded me, in moments when I couldn't believe in myself, that there is always a way forward.

A special thank you goes to my therapist, who has guided me with her expertise, empathy, and patience. She not only helped me understand myself better but also gave me the tools to cope with my fears.

Last but not least, I thank my contact person at the day clinic. Their support and commitment helped me take the first step toward healing. Their compassionate approach showed me that there are people who genuinely care and will catch me during difficult moments.

All of these people have helped me on my journey, strengthened and encouraged me, even when it wasn't easy. This book is as much a result of their belief in me as it is of my own strength. I am infinitely grateful to each and every one of you. ♥

With deepest gratitude,
Melina Schmuckli

References

Books and Literature

Bourne, Edmund J. *The Anxiety and Phobia Workbook*. New Harbinger Publications, 2015.
Wolf, Doris. *Ängste verstehen und überwinden: Ein Selbsthilfeprogramm in kognitiver Verhaltenstherapie*. PAL-Verlag, 2019.
Greenberger, Dennis, und Christine Padesky. *Mind Over Mood: Change How You Feel by Changing the Way You Think*. Guilford Press, 2016.
Anxiety A to Z von Tamryn J. Burgers, R.H.N.

Studies and Scientific Articles:

American Psychiatric Association. *Diagnostic and Statistical Manual of Mental Disorders (DSM-5®)*. American Psychiatric Publishing, 2013.
Hofmann, Stefan G., et al. „Cognitive Behavioral Therapy for Anxiety Disorders: A Meta-Analysis of Randomized Placebo-Controlled Trials.“ *JAMA Psychiatry*, 2012.

Digital Resources:

Deutsche Depressionshilfe. *Transkranielle Magnetstimulation (TMS)*. Zugriff unter: www.deutsche-depressionshilfe.de.
PsychCentral. „Coping with Anxiety and Depression.“ Zugriff unter: www.psychcentral.com.
MindDoc App. Zugriff unter: www.minddoc.de.

Apps and Programs:

> Headspace: Meditation und Achtsamkeit. Zugriff unter: www.headspace.com.
> Calm: Schlaf und Stressreduktion. Zugriff unter: www.calm.com.
> Selfapy: Online-Therapie. Zugriff unter: www.selfapy.de.

Personal Inspiration:

> Personal Experiences and Reflections, Enhanced by Conversations with Affected Individuals and Professionals:
> Sharing personal experiences, alongside insights from others who have walked similar paths, can provide a sense of connection and validation. It allows individuals to feel less alone and gain new perspectives on their own struggles. Reflecting on these experiences, while also learning from professionals in the field, can create a well-rounded approach to healing and growth. Below is a reflection on how personal experiences and insights from others have shaped my own journey and understanding of mental health challenges.

Links:

> https://www.gesundheitsinformation.de/behandlungsmoeglichkeiten-bei-generalisierter-angststoerung.html?utm_source=chatgpt.com

https://www.therapie.de/psyche/info/index/diagnose/angst/entspannung-sport-selbsthilfetipps/?utm_source=chatgpt.com

https://beavivo.de/magazin/angststoerung/?utm_source=chatgpt.com

https://www.enableme.de/de/artikel/panikattacken-angst-oder-depression-10438?utm_source=chatgpt.com

https://psychische-hilfe.wien.gv.at/betreuung/gesund-werden-und-bleiben-betreuung-bei-depressionen-oder-angststoerungen/?utm_source=chatgpt.com
https://www.welt.de/podcasts/aha-zehn-minuten-alltags-wissen/article255119932/Wissenschafts-Podcast-Wie-autogenes-Training-Stress-abbaut-und-Resilienz-staerkt.html?utm_source=chatgpt.com

https://www.aerzteblatt.de/nachrichten/154585/Apps-koennten-bei-generalisierten-Angststoerungen-helfen?utm_source=chatgpt.com

https://www.beltz.de/fachmedien/psychologie/produkte/details/55575-therapie-tools-angststoerungen.html?utm_source=chatgpt.com

https://www.psychotherapeut-linz.at/entspannungstechniken?utm_source=chatgpt.com

https://www.orthomol.com/de-de/lebenswelten/nerven-psyche-stress/stress-muedigkeit/entspannungstechniken?utm_source=chatgpt.com

https://blackroll.com/de/artikel/entspannungstechniken

https://www.apa.org/

https://www.nice.org.uk/

https://adaa.org/

https://hsph.harvard.edu/

https://www.sleepfoundation.org/

https://www.cdc.gov/

https://www.medizin.uni-tuebingen.de/de/tms-depression?utm_source=chatgpt.com

https://www.deutsche-depressionshilfe.de/forschungszentrum/aktuellestudien/transkranielle-magnetstimulation-tms?utm_source=chatgpt.com

About the Author

Melina Schmuckli was born on February 27, 1999, and is passionately engaged in the topic of mental health.

Through her own experiences with anxiety disorders, panic attacks, and PTSD, she knows how challenging the path to healing can be. Her goal is to inspire others who are affected and share valuable strategies that have helped her personally.

She originally trained as a businesswoman. In her free time, she enjoys spending time in nature, taking care of her raised bed and plants, or experimenting with new recipes in the kitchen. Her cats and her partner are particularly important to her and accompany her on her journey.

You can find more about her work on TikTok and Instagram under the name anxietyjournals.

Daily Journal

Below is an example of a daily journal that helped me recognize the small progress I made and learn to appreciate it.

I've attached a few pages so that, if you don't have a journal on hand or don't know what to write, you can start here.

Such journals are available in various styles, colors, and designs online. You can order them in paper form or download and print them.

It can be very important to note things that only become apparent when you look back at your journal at a later time, and you realize that you've already made some significant progress. These changes happen so gradually that you don't notice them.

Be proud of every step in the right direction, no matter how small, because you are strong and you can achieve anything!

Daily Planner

Date:____

Mood in the Morning (1-10):____________________

Daily Overview

Today's Goals:

____

Important to do's:

1.____

2.____

3.____

Today's Symptoms

Note how you feel physically and emotionally. Pay attention to specific symptoms of anxiety:

( ) Trembling

( ) Racing Heart

( ) Shortness of breath

( ) Nausea

( ) Dizziness

( ) Other:_______________________________

the severity of symptoms (1-10):________________

Notes

Have you noticed today? Are there things that worry you or that you'd like to share?

____

____

____

Self-care checklist

( ) A relaxing drink (e.g. Tea)

( ) A short walk outdoors

( ) Deep breathing (5-5-5 technique)

( ) Doing something creative, such as painting or writing

( ) A short meditation or practicing mindfulness

( ) Scheduling breaks

( ) Writing something positive, such as gratitude

Evening reflection

What went well today?_______________________________________

What could have gone better?_________________________________

How do you feel now?____

Daily Planner

Date:____

Mood in the Morning (1-10):_____________________

Daily Overview

Today's Goals:

____

Important to do's:

1.____

2.____

3.____

Today's Symptoms

Note how you feel physically and emotionally. Pay attention to specific symptoms of anxiety:

( ) Trembling

( ) Racing Heart

( ) Shortness of breath

( ) Nausea

( ) Dizziness

( ) Other:_______________________________________

the severity of symptoms (1-10):_________________

Notes

Have you noticed today? Are there things that worry you or that you'd like to share?

____

____

____

Self-care checklist

( ) A relaxing drink (e.g. Tea)

( ) A short walk outdoors

( ) Deep breathing (5-5-5 technique)

( ) Doing something creative, such as painting or writing

( ) A short meditation or practicing mindfulness

( ) Scheduling breaks

( ) Writing something positive, such as gratitude

Evening reflection

What went well today?_______________________________

What could have gone better?___________________________

How do you feel now?________________________________

Daily Planner

Date:____

Mood in the Morning (1-10):___________________

Daily Overview

Today's Goals:

____

Important to do's:

1.____

2.____

3.____

Today's Symptoms

Note how you feel physically and emotionally. Pay attention to specific symptoms of anxiety:

( ) Trembling

( ) Racing Heart

( ) Shortness of breath

( ) Nausea

( ) Dizziness

( ) Other:_______________________________

the severity of symptoms (1-10):_______________

Notes

Have you noticed today? Are there things that worry you or that you'd like to share?

____

____

____

Self-care checklist

( ) A relaxing drink (e.g. Tea)

( ) A short walk outdoors

( ) Deep breathing (5-5-5 technique)

( ) Doing something creative, such as painting or writing

( ) A short meditation or practicing mindfulness

( ) Scheduling breaks

( ) Writing something positive, such as gratitude

Evening reflection

What went well today?_______________________________

What could have gone better?_______________________

How do you feel now?_______________________________

Daily Planner

Date:____

Mood in the Morning (1-10):___________________

Daily Overview

Today's Goals:

____

Important to do's:

1.____

2.____

3.____

Today's Symptoms

Note how you feel physically and emotionally. Pay attention to specific symptoms of anxiety:

( ) Trembling

( ) Racing Heart

( ) Shortness of breath

( ) Nausea

( ) Dizziness

( ) Other:_________________________________

the severity of symptoms (1-10):_______________

Notes

Have you noticed today? Are there things that worry you or that you'd like to share?

____

____

____

Self-care checklist

( ) A relaxing drink (e.g. Tea)

( ) A short walk outdoors

( ) Deep breathing (5-5-5 technique)

( ) Doing something creative, such as painting or writing

( ) A short meditation or practicing mindfulness

( ) Scheduling breaks

( ) Writing something positive, such as gratitude

Evening reflection

What went well today?_______________________________

What could have gone better?_______________________

How do you feel now?_______________________________

Daily Planner

Date:_______________________________________

Mood in the Morning (1-10):__________________

Daily Overview

Today's Goals:

____

Important to do's:

1._______________________________________

2._______________________________________

3._______________________________________

Today's Symptoms

Note how you feel physically and emotionally. Pay attention to specific symptoms of anxiety:

( ) Trembling

( ) Racing Heart

( ) Shortness of breath

( ) Nausea

( ) Dizziness

( ) Other:_______________________________

the severity of symptoms (1-10):______________

Notes

Have you noticed today? Are there things that worry you or that you'd like to share?

____

____

____

Self-care checklist

( ) A relaxing drink (e.g. Tea)

( ) A short walk outdoors

( ) Deep breathing (5-5-5 technique)

( ) Doing something creative, such as painting or writing

( ) A short meditation or practicing mindfulness

( ) Scheduling breaks

( ) Writing something positive, such as gratitude

Evening reflection

What went well today?_______________________________

What could have gone better?_______________________

How do you feel now?_______________________________

Daily Planner

Date:_______________________________________

Mood in the Morning (1-10):___________________

Daily Overview

Today's Goals:

____

Important to do's:

1._______________________________________

2._______________________________________

3._______________________________________

Today's Symptoms

Note how you feel physically and emotionally. Pay attention to specific symptoms of anxiety:

( ) Trembling

( ) Racing Heart

( ) Shortness of breath

( ) Nausea

( ) Dizziness

( ) Other:___________________________________

the severity of symptoms (1-10):_______________

Notes

Have you noticed today? Are there things that worry you or that you'd like to share?

____

____

____

Self-care checklist

( ) A relaxing drink (e.g. Tea)

( ) A short walk outdoors

( ) Deep breathing (5-5-5 technique)

( ) Doing something creative, such as painting or writing

( ) A short meditation or practicing mindfulness

( ) Scheduling breaks

( ) Writing something positive, such as gratitude

Evening reflection

What went well today?_______________________________

What could have gone better?_______________________

How do you feel now?_______________________________

Daily Planner

Date:____

Mood in the Morning (1-10):___________________

Daily Overview

Today's Goals:

____

Important to do's:

1.____

2.____

3.____

Today's Symptoms

Note how you feel physically and emotionally. Pay attention to specific symptoms of anxiety:

( ) Trembling

( ) Racing Heart

( ) Shortness of breath

( ) Nausea

( ) Dizziness

( ) Other:_______________________________

the severity of symptoms (1-10):_____________

Notes

Have you noticed today? Are there things that worry you or that you'd like to share?

____

____

____

Self-care checklist

( ) A relaxing drink (e.g. Tea)

( ) A short walk outdoors

( ) Deep breathing (5-5-5 technique)

( ) Doing something creative, such as painting or writing

( ) A short meditation or practicing mindfulness

( ) Scheduling breaks

( ) Writing something positive, such as gratitude

Evening reflection

What went well today?____

What could have gone better?____________________________________

How do you feel now?____

Daily Planner

Date:____

Mood in the Morning (1-10):__________________

Daily Overview

Today's Goals:

____

Important to do's:

1.____

2.____

3.____

Today's Symptoms

Note how you feel physically and emotionally. Pay attention to specific symptoms of anxiety:

( ) Trembling

( ) Racing Heart

( ) Shortness of breath

( ) Nausea

( ) Dizziness

( ) Other:____

the severity of symptoms (1-10):________________

Notes

Have you noticed today? Are there things that worry you or that you'd like to share?

____

____

____

Self-care checklist

( ) A relaxing drink (e.g. Tea)

( ) A short walk outdoors

( ) Deep breathing (5-5-5 technique)

( ) Doing something creative, such as painting or writing

( ) A short meditation or practicing mindfulness

( ) Scheduling breaks

( ) Writing something positive, such as gratitude

Evening reflection

What went well today?_______________________________

What could have gone better?_______________________

How do you feel now?_______________________________

Daily Planner

Date:____

Mood in the Morning (1-10):___________________

Daily Overview

Today's Goals:

____

Important to do's:

1.____

2.____

3.____

Today's Symptoms

Note how you feel physically and emotionally. Pay attention to specific symptoms of anxiety:

( ) Trembling

( ) Racing Heart

( ) Shortness of breath

( ) Nausea

( ) Dizziness

( ) Other:_______________________________________

the severity of symptoms (1-10):________________

Notes

Have you noticed today? Are there things that worry you or that you'd like to share?

____

____

____

Self-care checklist

( ) A relaxing drink (e.g. Tea)

( ) A short walk outdoors

( ) Deep breathing (5-5-5 technique)

( ) Doing something creative, such as painting or writing

( ) A short meditation or practicing mindfulness

( ) Scheduling breaks

( ) Writing something positive, such as gratitude

Evening reflection

What went well today?_______________________________

What could have gone better?_______________________

How do you feel now?_______________________________

Daily Planner

Date:____

Mood in the Morning (1-10):___________________

Daily Overview

Today's Goals:

____

Important to do's:

1.____

2.____

3.____

Today's Symptoms

Note how you feel physically and emotionally. Pay attention to specific symptoms of anxiety:

( ) Trembling

( ) Racing Heart

( ) Shortness of breath

( ) Nausea

( ) Dizziness

( ) Other:_______________________________________

the severity of symptoms (1-10):________________

Notes

Have you noticed today? Are there things that worry you or that you'd like to share?

____

____

____

Self-care checklist

( ) A relaxing drink (e.g. Tea)

( ) A short walk outdoors

( ) Deep breathing (5-5-5 technique)

( ) Doing something creative, such as painting or writing

( ) A short meditation or practicing mindfulness

( ) Scheduling breaks

( ) Writing something positive, such as gratitude

Evening reflection

What went well today?________________________________

What could have gone better?____________________________

How do you feel now?________________________________